Waiting for Service

An Insider's account of Why Customer Service is Broken + Tips to avoid bad service

Waiting for Service
Copyright 2021
All rights reserved.
Publisher: Bien Publishing

In loving memory of my brother, Bobby.

Contents

INTRODUCTION 6
BAD BY DESIGN 8
    Making you wait is profitable 9
WAITING IN LINE AT THE BANK 11
    Outside in perspective 12
    Getting around the system 14
VISITING THE POST OFFICE 15
    Getting around the system 16
WALMART 17
    Getting around the system 18
MCDONALD'S 19
    How to get better service at the Drive-throughs 20
AIRLINES 21
    Getting around the system 22
CUSTOMER SERVICE IS AN AFTERTHOUGHT 23
YOUR CALL IS VERY IMPORTANT TO US, BUT 25
CITIZEN SERVICES DESIGNED TO
DISAPPOINT YOU 27
    The Taliban now has customer service 28
IN DEFENSE OF THE AGENCY EMPLOYEES 30
    How do you get help? 32
WHY SUPERVISORS ARE NEVER AVAILABLE 34
WHY DO I HAVE TO FILL OUT ALL THESE
FORMS TO GET A REBATE? 36
    How do you get around the rebate Olympics? 37
INTERNET SERVICE PROVIDERS 38
YOU CAN BE BAD AT CUSTOMER SERVICE
AND BE VERY PROFITABLE 42
YOUR LOCAL CONGRESSMAN
HAS BEEN PAID OFF 44

GIVING THEM MY MONEY IS EASY; GETTING IT BACK IS HARD	46
ANYTHING YOU SAY ON THIS CALL CAN AND WILL BE USED AGAINST YOU	48
THE LIES START EARLY AND OFTEN	50
HAS ALL TRUST WITH SERVICE ERODED?	52
CUSTOMER SERVICE FAILS SERVICE WORKERS EVEN MORE	54
EMPLOYEE FIRST, CUSTOMER SECOND	57
THOSE ANNOYING CHATBOTS	60
How to avoid chatbot pain	61
TECHNOLOGY HAS THE WHEEL	63
I CAN'T CALL A 1-800 # IN FRONT OF YOUNG CHILDREN	64
CONSULTANTS HAVE SOLD OUT TO BIG TECHNOLOGY COMPANIES	67
MRS. LINCOLN, OTHER THAN THAT, HOW DID YOU ENJOY THE PLAY?	70
OUTSOURCING OVERSEAS	75
WHAT CUSTOMER SUCCESS CAN TEACH US ABOUT CUSTOMER SERVICE	77
THE WAY FORWARD	80
Prosecution's closing argument against Customer Service	80
IN DEFENSE OF CUSTOMER SERVICE	86
THREE BOLD IDEAS FOR CUSTOMER SERVICE	88
Brutally honest expectation setting	88
CUSTOMER SERVICE ECONOMICS - PAY FOR SERVICE	91
CUSTOMER 'SERVICITIZATION'	93
GETTING AROUND CUSTOMER SERVICE	93
GOVERNMENT AGENCIES WORKAROUND	97
Where do we go from Here?	98

INTRODUCTION

It has been a nice career for me. I plan to tell the whole truth, and it won't be popular. I wrote this book because I had to. The truth is your favorite companies could fix customer service in one day if they really wanted to. They won't. and I know why.

I do not need to convince you that Customer service is broken. No need to take my word for it. I am simply saying it is raining bad service outside, go outside and see if you get wet. I've spent most of my career working with dozens of organizations that hired me to help them fix customer service. I haven't been all that successful. Some areas in customer service are getting worse. I've written extensively about the matter but erroneously wrote to the people in charge of fixing customer service. I gave them blueprints, know-how, and shared everything I knew, to no avail. This time I'm writing to you, the customer—the one who votes with your wallet. I've had a 2 decade career in the customer service industry, and I'm going to share information about the industry that may make you uneasy. I'll answer your burning questions and give you tips on how to get better service. I also plan to share a few radical ideas on what the future should look like.

I suspect that many of my colleagues will not take my calls when I'm done, but I plan to lay it out bare nonetheless.

One more possible outcome is that I may never get another job in this industry after this book is published, so please buy more than one copy if you can. Spread the Gospel. Join the Revolution at waitingforservice.com

BAD BY DESIGN

Your customer service experience isn't bad by accident. Most of it was intentionally built to be mediocre. There are many reasons for this but more on that later.

On hold with AT&T for an hour, and still no resolution. 10 years of loyalty, and I feel more like a burden. I called to explain my issue and was on hold for 45 mins when the call dropped. Rinse and repeat! Time to find another carrier.

I am starting with your ability to even reach customer service, or as I call it, the front gate. The most common complaint I hear about service is wait time. We all complain about long wait times over the phone or waiting for someone to respond on chat or email. This complaint is several decades old and seems to be getting worse. As I write this, the wait time for my internet broadband company was over 45 minutes on the phone yesterday, and I was 14th in line waiting on chat. I wrote while on hold and followed the race between telephone and chat. Telephone won out. I spoke with a young lady named Misty. She was polite but ultimately couldn't help me, so she transferred me to someone else. I couldn't see what she was doing on her end, but she must have sent me to the "hang up on you" department because that was what happened. I ended up getting service going through the back door, and I'll be sharing tips to help you navigate this world of customer service till we make good service the norm.

The average American will wait on hold for 43 days throughout a lifetime.

Making you wait is profitable

If you want to talk to a human being, it costs the company money to talk to you. There are two main drivers in that cost—wages and tech. More on the tech later, but the main reason you have any long wait times is that they don't want to pay to shorten your wait time. To be fair, there are several reasons why they can't or won't pay to reduce your wait time, but it almost always comes down to money.

The sun looked almost orange like it was mad at us. We were in the pacific northwest, and the temperature was 104, but my client insisted on having the meeting outdoors. I was there on their campus for one reason—to fix the customer experience. I'd be meeting with Terry one-on-one to preview the report of my findings before I shared it with the rest of the team.

He wiped the sweat off his brow and asked, "How bad is it?" in his Texan drawl.

I said, "Do you want the bad news or the worse news?"

He was a bottom-line guy, so I skipped the preamble and flipped to the page with the key data. I said that, on average, his customers would want to wait 52 seconds when they called his store, but it was currently averaging 619 seconds. I then gave him three options, and this is where you, the consumer, need to pay attention.

He could hire more people to respond to customers and lower the wait time, or he could use technology to reduce the wait time by moving customers towards options that wouldn't require a person, or he could do a hybrid of both. Each of these three options has some cost associated with it, but the human option is always the most expensive.

Terry leaned in and said, "I think option 2 is a no-brainer. These are low-value inquiries; we just need to automate them. Or do you think I'm crazy?"

I made a mental calculation every person in my profession has made many times. *Do I tell him the truth, or do I need another check from him?*

So I said, "You're not crazy, especially if your brand is all about low friction."

I was trying to justify the decision we both knew was at best rushed, at worst plain wrong.

How much more expensive? Consider that to even temporarily give his customers what they wanted would cost him an incremental 9 million dollars annually. So for him, that was a non-starter. This option is always a non-starter. In my 20 years of doing this, not one single client has ever taken this option. I rarely push this option. Most consultants don't even explore the obvious answer. What you need to understand about consultants is that they are expensive, so if a company is willing to just spend the money and improve your service, they may not need my help. Terry hired me so he could deliver service to you at the lowest possible price. Standing between you and shorter wait times is $9M a year to the bottom line. You have no chance.

WAITING IN LINE AT THE BANK

"One cashier, long lines, and accounts in your name you're unaware of."

You'd think the best service for you is in-person service since we've been doing in-person customer service for thousands of years. If you somehow think this means we've gotten good at it, you would be wrong.

I was in a small lake town outside West Palm Beach. I had been hired by a regional bank to do the only thing people hire me to do—fix the customer experience. There were plenty of problems, but on the list was this issue of the in-person experience. Like I always do, my team and I spoke to customers. What the bank said the customers wanted and what they really wanted differed greatly. For one thing, the bank thought customers wanted better technology from their bank. Their actual customers wanted to get their issue resolved by a person, and if they were bringing technology instead, it must be superior to a person.

I should state that often when companies hire me and my team, they already have a theory of the case—an idea they believe will improve customer service. They're hiring me mostly to confirm their bias and then turn the idea into an actual plan.

The folks from this bank were no different. They kept telling me their customers wanted better tech and a better banking app. Their chief security officer said, "If I were you, I'd just look at what Chase is doing and see how we can do something like that."

This is what happens when company executives mistake customer Preferences for customer preferences. I have a preference when it comes to eating at a restaurant. I generally prefer a table over a booth, but that will be a lower-case preference for me. On the other hand, I want a hot meal and a clean table, so if they have to put me in a booth to get me a clean table, it won't be that big a deal. On the other hand, if they make me wait for an hour just to get me a booth, they will have failed.

Outside in perspective

We did talk to their customers. None wanted the bank to look anything like Chase. Many of them chose the bank because it was the opposite of what they imagined J.P Morgan Chase to be. They wanted human contact. This didn't mean they didn't want smart, effective technology. It was not a mutually exclusive choice. Above all, they wanted to feel like they mattered and not just a number. I shared some quotes from their customers. They included "what happened to service," "we can never talk to a person," "your phone menu is confusing." I was met with resistance and presented with other research that supported their bias towards adding more tech.

I made it a point to sit directly across from their CEO. I wanted to read his expressions. My colleague went over the findings and our recommendation. The CEO had a look on his face of a man who'd just received unexpected and dire news from his oncologist. He was unsettled because the reason he hired me and my team was in the hope we would tell him what he wanted to hear—that there was a way to keep his customers happy by not giving them what they asked for.

Why did he not want to give them what they asked for? Money. Round and round we go. This will come up a lot.

The bank sees this as a struggle for survival. They're losing customers to the competition and desperately trying to save money. In their quest to conserve capital, the customer experience suffers.

Twenty years ago, traffic to the physical bank peaked and has since been on the decline. So they scaled back the number of employees per branch, and while this saved money, it increased wait times. Compounding this problem is that as they reduced staff at the physical location, they failed to increase staff at their customer interaction center (call center). As more customers were forced to use the phone and online chat to resolve issues, their wait time began to grow longer. Instead of hiring more staff, the bank created more friction for its customers. First, they built an automated phone system so they would not have to talk to customers. Then they kept adding more menu options to make a bad system more "efficient." Predictably, all this did was accelerate the customer exodus, which accelerated their revenue losses—a condition we call circling the drain.

This moment is when a strong CEO becomes critical. One who understands that the riskiest bets are the ones that appear safe. Customer service doesn't need to be expensive, but it costs money, and if you do it correctly, there is a return on your investments.

We gave him the course of action to take. It involved hiring more people and using technology in smarter ways but never at the expense of the customer. He asked for an alternate plan. We told him we were already in the middle of the alternate plan. The alternate plan was the status quo.

Getting around the system

The financial incentives are set up for your service to be bad. People optimize for what's in their best interest. The executives and shareholders of the bank want to keep customers happy and make a profit, but if they have to choose, they pick profits every time. So as you navigate support at the bank, think about what you need and what channel you should use wisely. In general, if you need something quick, easy, and informational, lean on technology—apps and websites. If your need is going to take some time, you want a person. We'll cover in-depth some tips to make getting a person easier, but what you want to do is find where the companies' pressure points are. For most companies, it's social media. This is where they feel so much pressure that they devote more resources, and you can often get faster service.

VISITING THE POST OFFICE

USPS made me wait three hours in line only to lose my package and no one to help me.

The post office seems to be trying to be good at customer service, but they're still failing. I know they're trying to be good because they have a massive banner in their offices that says they care about the customer experience. Yet, they proceed to make you wait for hours and deal with rude employees.

I don't have intimate knowledge of the USPS, but from publicly available financials, it's clear they're struggling. When I look at the value proposition of sending a piece of mail, I pay less than 50 cents and expect the mail to travel thousands of miles on time. I suspect we're all still amazed that you can get a piece of mail from New York to LA for under $0.50, and given that the USPS is losing billions every year, my guess is no one can survive under those pricing conditions. What does this have to do with service? Well, customer service costs money. Let me say that again: customer service costs money. The USPS needs to be as lean as possible. They're bleeding money, so they can't afford more cashiers. What they'll do instead is hire someone like me to help them deliver just enough service—not enough to please the customers, but enough to prevent them from showing up with pitchforks at their offices.

What you get instead are platitudes promising great customer service and technology designed only to save the company money by forcing you to interact with it even if you're frustrated. If the United States Post office wanted to deliver on its promises, it'd lose many customers. Anyone with a basic understanding of economics gets the competitive disadvantage the organization is under because of its ultra-low prices. The USPS would have to increase revenue through price hikes to fund the customer service transformation. The question is: how many of us are willing to pay a lot more?

Getting around the system

Please shop elsewhere or write your congressman or woman to raise prices. If you want marginally better service, pay extra at their competitors. Their competitors aren't great, but they are better and usually significantly more expensive. You get what you pay for. Your move!

WALMART

"Save money and live better!" Looks like an old wound.

When you're unable to find what you're looking for and there's no one around to ask, then you check yourself out and pack your bags.

One shopper fell, hit, and bruised their head on the way down and was dizzy. Asked for help with 911. The staff said the bruising looks like an old wound.

I'm old enough to remember where it was a rarity to bag your groceries. Now it's commonplace. It's not inconceivable that we'll eventually be doing inventory at Walmart. I mean we're not that far away from someone handing you the keys to a forklift to go retrieve your boxes of cereal from the top shelf, then place it in your cart, scan, bag, and pay for it yourself. As you leave the store, scan your receipt again so Walmart makes sure you didn't steal anything.

On a serious note, how did we get here? How is the largest employer in the US incapable of delivering the basics of customer service? How do they continue to have fiercely loyal customers? After all, even Walmart haters hate on Walmart from inside of Walmart as they begrudgingly hand Walmart their wallets. What is at play here?

As much as I'd like to pile on here, I think this is a case of mistaken identity. You see, when you stepped into Walmart, you might have misunderstood the value proposition. Walmart has never been loud about how great it is at customer service. All it promotes is its price. I appreciate the honesty. Part of the service they're offering is helpful staff and clean stores, but they've never been good at it, and it hasn't hurt them. Again—you get what you pay for.

Walmart is arguably one of the more consumer-friendly brands out there. They maniacally focus on price and believe their customers are willing to forgive everything else. This formula has made Walmart wealthy beyond imagination, giving the internet plenty to laugh about and, in my mind, a good deal for its customers.

Getting around the system

You can ask for a manager or escalate Customer Service at Walmart and anywhere else, but it's a rookie playbook from the 90s. Even the kids call that being a "Karen."

What works is engaging the corporate office. When you have a wrong at the local store and can't get help, head over to the corporate offices. You don't need to fly to Arkansas. All you need is a dial-up connection OR a flip phone. Start with social media—Twitter is a good place for this.

MCDONALD'S

They couldn't even say please and thank you when it wasn't busy. The store is xxxxxxxx. Rude as hell. Can't say please or thank you during the order. Said these people don't need their job there. They blow.

Drive-throughs have a bad reputation, and I know why. I'm still amazed that almost 100 years have passed since we came up with this beautiful concept—combining the joy of traffic with food you can eat with one hand while you drive with the other hand. Apparently, this mobile culinary miracle isn't enough. We also want to be treated nicely. We're such a demanding bunch!

The clue to this problem is in the name. Fast food, not great food, or friendly food. Fast is the promise. That said, it's a low bar to at least be courteous. We can't blame this entirely on money. So what's at play here? Why won't these multinational companies at least just copy what Chick-Fil-A's doing with their please and thank you?

In defense of McDonald's or whoever else, they are pretty fast. Have you cooked a burger in 30 seconds before? Their priorities are focused on profits—you know, marketing, the enticing burgers, speed of delivery. Do you know what isn't as profitable? Spending money on extra training or paying a tiny bit more for better staff.

We did some work for one of the largest fast-food chains in the U.S. three years ago. After landing at their headquarters in the Midwest, I was struck by how nice the offices were. When you think about their brand as a consumer, you think cheap.

You forget these are multi-billion dollar corporations with deep pockets. The reason I'm here, as you might have guessed, is to look into customer service. The problem they wanted to solve was to reduce how much customer service was costing them. I couldn't believe my ears. They wanted to spend LESS on customer service. I typed their name into my social media listening software. They had 7300+ mentions that day alone, most of them negative. I looked at the economics of their business, focusing on the service side. Customer service was a nuisance for them. Any savings went straight to the bottom line. So while you complain about service, they think there's an opportunity to save money. Remember this most customer service is about customer mollification, not satisfaction. What they and other companies are doing is to add more and more technology to keep you mollified. The vision is to spend more on technology to automate most of the experience. This is not a crazy plan. The problem is in the execution—the use of technology in place of a person isn't necessarily bad when it's well thought out.

How to get better service at the Drive-throughs

When heading to the drive-through, some rules can help make the experience better for you. Try to be pleasant to all employees. They're handling your food, and most of the problem with your experience isn't their fault. Opt out of bad technology early and often. This is a feedback loop. The more customers suffer through bad technology, the more the companies keep them in place. If, on the other hand, most customers opt out, they'll have no choice but to improve or dump it. If you must talk to a manager, do not be a jerk. The manager is probably on your side but has limited options. The best thing to do if you feel you've been wronged is to talk to the corporate office. Flip to the Fighting Back chapter to read and follow the playbook.

AIRLINES

If you get to the check-in desk too early to ensure baggage check-in, you can expect to be treated with rudeness. If your flight is delayed or rescheduled, don't expect anything—no credit, no discounts, no apologies. You will be granted free water and soda.

@Delta I can't believe I've been waiting three hours on hold to tell you I'm traveling with an 11-week-old puppy on my return flight. You took my $1500 in less than 10 minutes, yet can't be bothered to render reasonable customer service. You suck.

For most of my adult life, I was on a plane at least every other week. I used to say I was stuck in an abusive relationship with American Airlines. There are many issues with airlines, but let's focus on the most frustrating part—all the waiting. What's up with all the waiting? If you've flown in the last ten years, this will seem familiar. You start your day at the airport security lines and where things start to go awry. The first thing you notice is the very long line to talk to a gate agent, then the line to get through security. While we can blame the TSA for some of this bulk, some of the blame belongs to the airlines. Then there's the wait to board, then the wait to take off, and on and on it goes....

Ten years ago, I was consulting for one of the largest airlines. An essential part of the conversation was about luggage. They were trying to stimulate revenue because they were historically not profitable. One way of doing that was raising fees by charging customers what used to be included in the ticket price. My team and I went out and researched the trade-off: how much revenue could be generated from forcing customers to have to check in their bags for a fee? What we found was that charging the fee created friction for the customers who paid the baggage fees, but it had an even more insidious side effect. It degraded the experience for all customers. By making people pay to check in their bags, most people opted to carry on to save the fee, and thus the majority of fliers brought their luggage through security, which accounted by one study for up 40% of the wait time.

Making matters worse is the fact that there was an easier way for them to get the revenue without the bad side effects. We recommended they instead charge people to carry on—people like me who travel for a living would pay to avoid checking in a bag. Charge business travelers the fees, and checking in will be faster; they get their revenue, and no one is harmed. They declined this option in part because they feared that if their competitors didn't also charge the same fee to business, travelers might lose profitable businesses. They opted to get more revenue by passing on the frustration to their customers.

Getting around the system

If you want to avoid waiting at the airport, take a car, because no one gets out of the airport without waiting. There are things to do to minimize your wait, but it'll cost you. For starters, buy an all-inclusive ticket that gives you the flexibility to check bags and pick your seat. Additionally, imagine your flight is late; there's a long line of people waiting to ask the service employee if the plane is coming. You can choose to waste your time waiting in line or waste even more time calling an 1800#, or you can simply get the information yourself from publicly available websites that track your incoming and outgoing flights and sometimes tell you where your plane is before the airline employees know. For more tips, go to the tips section where I talk about giving you back control.

CUSTOMER SERVICE IS AN AFTERTHOUGHT

I will never use them again. You have the worst customer service. The operator was extremely rude, 45 mins on hold for 3 days straight and constantly told you are 'next in line.'

If you pay attention, you'd realize that, somehow, the bigger the company, the worse they are at the phone. How does this 100-year-old technology stump the big guys but not small companies? As companies get more sophisticated, they're also more likely to follow the same path.

Even at the most profitable companies, customer service is on the bottom rung, maybe one rung above the janitorial services. I spent most of my adult life in and around customer service jobs. I know this to be true. Even as a senior customer service executive, I had to muscle my way to the big boys' table.

It is not that every company is evil. It's because most customer service departments are not set up to activate the brain's reward center. What do I mean? Compare customer service to marketing. In marketing, the saying goes, "Half of all money I spend on advertising is wasted, but I can't tell you which half." Marketing executives routinely brag about setting half their budget on fire but yet continue to get more and more resources. Meanwhile, the customer service department is strapped for cash.

What is different? Think of marketing as offense and customer service as a defense. Think marketing as Messi—the greatest soccer player ever, and think of customer service as a goalie. Even though Messi goes 1 for 4 on his shots on goal, every goal he scores activates the fans' reward center of the brain. That's why we want Messi to keep shooting. As for the Goalie, it's all relief when he makes a save. There's no jubilation, just relief.

Try this next time you have a long hold: go to the company site and contact 'sales.' Not 'service.' 'Sales.' In other words, tell the company you'd like to be separated from your money. I assure you the wait time will magically disappear or be significantly less. Remember: customer service is generally for customers who already paid—no reward.

YOUR CALL IS VERY IMPORTANT TO US, BUT...

My uncle used to say, "Only paying attention to everything before the word 'but' is BS." He was right then and is right here. If your call was that important, they'd be talking to you instead of making you wait.

Customer service teams have a difficult job. It's a complex puzzle to put together to make sure you can reach them when you want. It starts with the randomness of call arrival. It's impossible to predict when you may have a problem that warrants contacting customer service. So as you can imagine—while it's easy to predict when Customer Service will contact you, when they might do so remains the challenge. Customer Service is where most companies go to cut costs. They will not provide the resources needed to provide adequate service.

While you want to contact customer service about your issue at 8:30 pm after you put the kids to bed, the company you need to reach has other plans. They've decided they can only be open for nine hours a day, and those hours are 8-5, which happens to be when you're at work. That creates a bottleneck when many customers call on their lunch breaks. Still, the company has the same staff allocation as it does throughout the day. Maybe they should hire more staff? No—they wrongly concluded that customer service doesn't have a tangible return on investment. You'll receive platitudes like, "Your call is very important" or "We will be right with you."

There's a solution to this problem. It involves matching supply and demand. They could staff up at times when customers are most likely to call and extend hours of operations. Those pragmatic ideas cost money, and company customer service is mostly a cost with no ROI (or is it?).

In search of answers, they hire a consultant, someone like me, and my marching orders are usually to resolve the problem at the cheapest possible costs. This ends up being an end around the problem. One popular play is to use technology not to solve the wait but instead make the hold feel better. There's a long wait when someone comes on and says, "We can hold your place in line…"

You'll still have to wait an hour, but you can now multitask while you wait without listening to hold music—a sometimes tolerable way to avoid the essence of inadequate Customer Service.

CITIZEN SERVICES DESIGNED TO DISAPPOINT YOU

We were in a dimly lit conference room with a projector from the 1980s. Even the women were all in suits. After trying for 10 minutes to get the presentation to appear, we decided to have copies printed by one of their assistants. I was there to present my findings of the state of the agency responsible for unemployment benefits for millions of citizens. I intended to embarrass them when I got to the part about customer wait times by pointing out that the average wait time to initiate benefits was two hours. I was ready to browbeat them until, to my surprise, the man in charge confidently said, "I don't know about you, but if it's two hours standing between me and feeding my kids, I'll wait four hours!"

I knew right then and there that I was on a fool's errand. We can make some changes around the margins, but lasting change will take years. Maybe it's human nature's tendency to 'cut corners'?

I've recently completed two customer service strategies, design, and implementation for three agencies in two states. Close your eyes and imagine the worst customer service at any company you've done business with. Now imagine that you have no choice but to wait as long as they make you and put up with any rudeness you confront. Unlike your long wait time for the delivery of the furniture you bought, this is about getting your unemployment check to pay your rent.

On the inside are underpaid employees who have good intentions but eventually succumb to the bureaucracy and learned helplessness that grips most agencies. Combine that with the fact that there's little interagency coordination. There are competing factions within the same agency, and this makes it near impossible to get the services the citizens are owed.

Here's some good news: they're now flush with cash from the federal government specifically earmarked to bring citizen services up to date. Unfortunately, much of the money is already being wasted, but there's progress. Most states are leaning into being digital-first—they're putting greater emphasis on the websites and mobile apps. This is directionally positive, but before we see dramatic changes, much work needs to be done. From someone working with several of these agencies, it's going to be a while before you can expect even mediocre service.

The Taliban now has customer service

I'm writing this the same week the Taliban took back control of the Afghan government. What struck me is that even the Taliban is promising a Better Citizen experience. They published a phone number to call the government to register complaints. I decided to give them a long-distance call. I can't comment about the quality of service, but the speed is 50 times faster than calling the Oklahoma Department of Safety.

The system is designed to fail you. Agencies were built to put obstacles in the way of citizens. The roadblocks you and I experience are often a feature, not a defect. While that may make some sense in certain areas of the government, it makes zero sense when the agency in essence is an organization dedicated to serving the needs of its constituents. What we need is less friction, not more bureaucracy. The default state of governmental agencies is inertia.

The recent pandemic put a finer point on this century-long problem—when they were forced to shut down physical offices, the deficiencies in the system were further exposed. The issue is bigger than customer service and gets into the issue of fairness. There are ways to navigate the system and get the services if you know what you're doing. As a society, I do worry about setting up a hunger games system where your access to government services has everything to do with your technical savvy or your proximity to a physical office. The social contract we have as a society is to provide services for our neighbors when they're in need, regardless of education or zip code.

IN DEFENSE OF THE AGENCY EMPLOYEES

We were one of the first to arrive at 7:00 am, and each of us grabbed a number at the kiosk, and just to let you know... this place likes to taaake -- it -- slowww...

There was only one lady working the desk for about an hour before more help arrived close to 8:00. I would guess that by that time, there were 40-50 people waiting in the lobby.

By the time my husband's number was called, ALEC assisted him and told me to go back in the lobby and that he would call me once he was finished with my husband since they could only service one person at a time. I waited, and when he was finished, I returned to ALEC, and he told me to wait at least another 30-45 min, and that he would put my name back in the system to be called.

ARE YOU SERIOUS, ALEC???? I have been waiting for over an hour and a half, and my number was right behind my husband's number. I guess ALEC just wanted to feel empowered at the moment instead of delivering fair and decent customer service... ALEC also offered for me to go online, and I told him we did, but they offered services that had no wait time all the way in Oklahoma City!! WTH! That is over an hour away!! ALEC said the reason why it's that far is because it's all booked up.

Well, geez, ALEC... How much more can I be inconvenienced??!

There was no consideration. All this experience was about bad customer service. Nothing else.

I want to talk about the rampant apathy that is the stereotype of the governmental employee. I had zero understanding of why the default state of most employees you interact with ranged from apathy to downright rude. The obvious answer is simple: like every dysfunctional organization, the best people tend to leave, and the worst people stay.

I wanted to understand this deeper. So over the years, my team and I have now interviewed dozens of these public service employees. Close your eyes and imagine that you have a passion for helping kids, and you decide that the best way you can contribute is to work in child welfare. I met a young lady with this ambition; she showed up to the focus group with a tee-shirt that said *"unbothered"* and said to me that she "works her wage." She was underpaid and did enough to not get fired.

We found, on average, it takes only 120 days for employees to go from idealistic to jaded. Before you pass judgment, it is hard to exaggerate how demoralizing it is to work at a place that is set up for failure. Think about the space between your seats in your car and the console. The fact that someone consciously designed every car in the world to have a space big enough for your cell phone to get jammed in but not big enough for your fingers to reach it. It is my suspicion that whoever the genius behind that design created citizen services. It is designed to first and foremost frustrate you, and if you don't quit maybe you can reach your goal. The system fails its own employees every single day, and if you get them comfortable as I did, they will tell you no one cares. If you don't believe them, they have stories after stories of the system failing them and the citizens they are trying to help. None of this excuses the behavior, and it is not our fault that they work in a dysfunctional bureaucratic environment.

What happens when the company you are dealing with is not a company but a governmental agency? Who do you call when the cops are the ones robbing you? Outside of thoughts and prayers, let me offer some real help. What I have tried to do in this book is to strip the emotion out of the business of customer service and see it for what it is. The first thing to remember is that they are similar to most service organizations. The only difference is the reason your experience sucks has nothing to do with profit; you can replace profit with funding/budget/waste/fraud, and it is from the same tree.

So let's review some options; take the traditional advice for private companies I have provided with the following twists. Agencies are siloed—they do not talk to each other—so calling another agency is a waste of time. It is important to understand the motivations of the agencies and what moves them to act and what doesn't. Governmental agencies have no shame, so social media pressure has a very limited effect. They also tend to have only a couple of channels that actually work. It is usually in person or over the phone, and the rest of the options are sometimes too bad to even bother.

How do you get help?

So what do they respond to? Politics. Political pressure does work, but how? Remember that at the end of the day, whether the people are elected, appointed, or hired, it is a political organization. What this means for the services you need as a citizen is when the regular channel fails, and you need to escalate, do not waste your time with middle management or even upper management. Find the politician or the political appointee and contact them directly. You won't have to work too hard because they are public officials; they have to be accessible. In most cases, there is a "hotline" to report things; it is a good place to start. Next, find the contact information for your local congress representative or senator and the politician or political appointee over the agency in question. You want to reach out to both of them with very different messages. For the head of the agency, your message is specific and direct about your issue. For your legislator, the message should be focused on what they care about—re-election. Make it clear you vote, your family votes, you can influence other voters. Include specific details about your issue so that his office skips the entire line and gets your case to the top of the heap. Don't worry, your legislator will actually love to drag the agency to a hearing for some political theatre that helps them, you know, get re-elected. You need help from an agency that owes it to you; this is not the way I would design a system. It just is the way the system is. The local media is also a good place to go; while you may not watch the local news, lots of voters do—the reliable older voters still do.

WHY SUPERVISORS ARE NEVER AVAILABLE

Hello there. Spent 45 minutes on hold at Developer Services this morning. Briefly spoke to someone called 'Mark' who said his manager Darren would call me back today. He 'promised' that if Darren couldn't call and if there was no update, someone would call me as a 'courtesy.'

24 hours later, it comes as no surprise that no one called. Is this how you treat customers?

No manager wants to talk to a customer who asks for a manager. It's a fool's errand. There are only two kinds of "I want to speak to your manager." One is the pop culture phenomenon called "being a 'Karen'"—the unreasonable kind. The second is a reasonable customer caught up in a stupid policy or process. All managers and supervisors hate talking to either group, but it's the second group that is more frustrating because every policy of the company you find stupid or ridiculous, the managers find equally ridiculous.

I remember one incident over 20 years ago. A young lady in a yellow sundress walked over to my cubicle and asked, "Do you mind taking a sup call for me?"

I smiled. "I mind very much," then asked her to send me the caller. I introduced myself, and he proceeded to tell me what he wanted. I worked for a satellite company, and they'd introduced a station that was targeted at the LGBTQ community. The channel was a marketing gimmick like all the programming where popular movies and shows you find anywhere, but this man had an objection. He didn't have the subscription, but even the channel showing up in his menu was a bridge too far. I was called every name in the book. Anyone who's worked in customer service management has a similar story.

Managers aren't completely helpless in customer service. They have bad options. Let me explain what happens behind the scenes. You've lost your internet service, so you contact customer service hoping they'll solve your issue. Instead, the answer you get is that it'll take six days to send someone to fix it. Understandably, you channel your inner Karen (we all have it). You ask for a manager, assuming the manager takes your call. The manager is faced with some bad options to potentially help you. What you'd like is for the company you're paying for a service to drop everything and come resolve your issue. It should be that simple. But it isn't. Instead, since you're already a paying customer, the manager also has the policy to follow. They may have a little more autonomy than their employees, but you're not likely to get what you want. You'll be offered a half loaf. Please do not berate the employee. You'll get the most out of the manager call if you behave cordially. The manager knows it's ridiculous you have to wait days but doesn't have the authority to do more. If the compromise does not work for you, keep the manager on your side but ask to go higher up without alienating them.

WHY DO I HAVE TO FILL OUT ALL THESE FORMS TO GET A REBATE?

Let's take a detour and examine how customer service works in most companies. The customer service department is generally not involved in almost anything other than after something has gone wrong. Customer Service is the company janitor. The janitor didn't make the mess but is responsible for cleaning it.

If the company marketing department wanted to give you a $100 discount, they would've done so. The truth is they didn't want to give you a $100 discount. More accurately, they didn't want to give everyone a $100 discount. Instead, the rebate exists entirely as an endurance test. The smart calculation says that once there are enough obstacles to frustrate enough people, most will give up, and they give everyone an average of a lot less than a $100 rebate.

Why do organizations do this? Because it's profitable. Suppose you are the chief marketing officer for a wireless carrier, and you're looking to use the promotion to boost sales. Your budget is $50 per head, but you don't believe that's going to be enough to entice people. Since you can't increase the budget, you make the rebate/incentive $100 per head but build a labyrinth that only half the people are likely to get through. Voila! You can now have your cake and eat it too.

Many people sign up in part due to the generous rebate they won't receive because of the marketing hoops they have to jump through. When these customers realize they're not able to get their rebate, they call customer service. Customer service, not marketing. Customer service then takes the brunt and the blame. The janitor gets blamed if the toilets are dirty, whether they caused it or not.

How do you get around the rebate Olympics?

You have two choices. One is to not play in the rebate Olympics, meaning you just insist on getting your credit upfront. It's a powerful strategy, in part because, at the point of sale, you're not yet in the cheap arms of customer service. You're still in a position of strength. They don't have your money yet and want your sale. Ask for a statement credit instead or some other way of getting the $100 value instead of the rebate.

The second strategy is to focus on your endurance so you can medal in the Olympics. It comes down to persistence and some legwork. I recommend you engage the company for help. In many cases, they'll walk the walk with you and tell you exactly what to do to get your rebate. May the force be with you.

INTERNET SERVICE PROVIDERS

A Comcast rep renamed one of their clients from "Lisa Brown" to "Asshole Brown" in their internal system and then, oops, started sending out bills with that address on it. Don't worry, though; they swore it was an isolated incident and it wouldn't happen again.

And then other customers started sharing their stories. In a particularly classy case, they renamed a client to "Whore Julia" for complaining about the problems she was having with her service. But again, don't worry, just an isolated incident.

Cable and Internet service providers deserve a special place in customer service hell. Multiple sites are devoted to how much Comcast sucks. I could've written the entire book all about Comcast. Their work in customer abuse is remarkable. They're the Serena Williams, Michael Phelps, and Michael Jordan of bad customer service. If I sound like I'm drooling, it's because I am. What they've been able to pull off is quite remarkable.

I'll first share the bad news: unlike some of the many examples in this book, I'm not sure Comcast has few incentives to change unless you and I do something. Let me take you behind the scenes.

I was in the lobby of one of the largest cable/Internet service companies in the United States and was looking over my presentation one last time. I made some minor changes and closed my laptop. I got escorted into the conference room. Everyone was gathered and waiting. Ever the showman, I proceeded to dunk them pretty hard. I painted a bleak picture for them if they didn't do a few things to fix the customer experience. I talked about a world where consumers like you and me would be forced to look for other options. I'd given a version of this speech to executives from other industries. At this point, my audience is usually scared out of their minds, but not this time. I was the only one sweating because the presentation was not hitting the mark. No one was scared.

I started to wonder if I had gone to the wrong place. I was supposed to be addressing a company and an industry universally hated. The people who'd ask you to wait at home from 1-5 pm for a technician only for the technician to show up at 4:45 and not leave your house till 8 pm. They'd make you wait 7 hours. Cable turns the term loyalty on its head. The more loyal you are, the more you pay. They save their best prices and perks for the new suckers and punish you for being stupid enough to stick around. Why in God's green earth are they not scared to be pushed into oblivion?

Thankfully, one of their executives interrupted me and asked if he could share something with me. I obliged. He took over the monitor and proceeded to share how they were having the best year on record.

"What about customer churn?" I asked.

He replied that while they might have fewer customers than the year before, they simply raised prices on existing customers who continued to stay to make up the difference.

They own a dominant position as Internet service providers. Even if you cut the cord, you can't cut the cord. Where will you go? They'll just make up the difference using their monopoly.

He answered my question before I could ask it, which was, "What the heck was I hired to do?"

He said they were unhappy with their customer satisfaction scores. It was embarrassingly low, and they'd like to get it to a respectable score.

Customer Service is Rigged against You

YOU CAN BE BAD AT CUSTOMER SERVICE AND BE VERY PROFITABLE

- *Lawrence D. Armstrong • 12 days ago*

I just spent over 2 hours on the phone for nothing. You ask customers to troubleshoot and be your eyes in the field but are reluctant to send techs out to resolve, but when you do you want to charge astronomical prices and schedule multiple visits for different service issues (security and Wi-Fi). That's okay, after over 20 years of paying over $400 a month, I guess this is what I get for being crazy enough to be loyal.

I didn't do my homework before taking this gig, so I proceeded to study their business model and how it impacts customer experience. It's crucial to know that companies respond to economic pressures above all else. They generally don't do things intentionally that will impact their pocketbooks. The best way customers apply economic pressure is to fire the company and hire a competitor. This is where the story gets even darker. These companies have kneecapped their competition. Your congressional representative has helped them make sure your options are limited. Have you wondered why there isn't an overlap of cable providers? There is an agreement amongst them not to compete in the same market.

You can get internet with your phone company, but there are very few credible options. For most zip codes in America, the competition is usually between a bullet to the head (Comcast or their ilk) or poison (AT&T and their ilk).

That environment of monopoly allows for this kind of behavior. The customer is shackled by regulations and seedy backroom deals made by corporations and politicians. I don't believe the company condones changing a customer's name from Lisa Brown to A*&hole Brown, but there is a level of comfort knowing that your customers have nowhere to go that emboldens it.

Some brilliant people work at these organizations; I was an executive running customer service for one of the biggest players in this industry. Just in the same way, there are hard-working people at the DMV, but in the end, their incentives don't align with yours in any meaningful way to improve your service.

YOUR LOCAL CONGRESSMAN HAS BEEN PAID OFF

I wish we lived in a world with many options, but we don't. Certain zip codes have options, but the vast majority of us are limited to one provider. How do you get good service from a company that has no incentive to improve? Some technological advances will break this monopoly even if your congressman is still in the pocket of Big Cable.

When it comes to how much you pay, you must play the game, or you'll be screwed. If you're a current subscriber, your internet/cable service cost can be more than double what new subscribers pay. Make sure you stay a "new subscriber" forever.

Here's how to keep your abusive relationship fresh. You'll need a calendar reminder and some patience. If you find you're paying significantly higher than you used to when you were a new subscriber, pick up the phone and call the Internet service provider/cable company and calmly say your bill is too high. The representative will start throwing discounts at you. Listen with appreciation if it gets you close to your goal. Pay attention to the expiration dates on the discounts; they always have an expiration date. Make a note to call before they expire.

If the discounts are not generous enough, let them know you intend to cancel your service. They'll now send you to the retention or saves department. This department exists solely to mollify you with discounts and prevent you from leaving by discounting your services. Yes, it's a silly game they play, but they have kneecapped their competition, so here we are. When you get to the Saves group, you're going to have to put your poker face on. The representative on the line is here to give you the goodies, but you must play your part. This is largely performance art; the only way to get the biggest discounts is to truly act like you're going to discontinue your services. Keep haggling till you get the very best deal they can offer. This deal will also have an expiration date. Save the date on your calendar. You'll have to do this all over again, usually 12 months later.

Don't blame big cable/Internet providers. Blame your local government

We are hostages of the cable/Internet cartel. It doesn't have to be this way. The government can change that. There's a cycle of incumbent companies paying off your local government in a way that makes it impossible for competition. When was the last time you had a new player on the scene? I will wait. The only serious competition they have faced in my lifetime was a small company called Google, and they're only in a handful of cities and they were successful in stifling Google in many cities.

You're going to hear the incumbents talk about the investments they've made historically, and your local government wax poetic about "rights of way revenue". When in fact, they are colluding to make it impossible for true competition.

GIVING THEM MY MONEY IS EASY; GETTING IT BACK IS HARD

I ordered a custom hot tub during the pandemic from Wayfair. It was scheduled for delivery in 4 months. I wasn't happy about the timing but decided to live with it until I saw an email from them that said the delivery would be in 10 months. I went to their website to use online chat—we can have a documented written conversation. Their policy didn't allow them to cancel an order that wouldn't be delivered for another 10 months. Without any prompting, the representative suggested I speak to a manager. Now I had to place a phone call. After a 47 minute wait, the manager said he needed a few days to rectify the situation. They continue to hold on to my $4,000, but I hope to get it back soon.

Why does placing an order take considerably less effort than getting your money back? Because it's profitable. Remember the playbook for rebates: the organization makes getting your rebate a bit more challenging so that only the fittest survive. Same play here.

The calculus is simple: make the policies that are good for the company easy, the ones that are good for you but bad for them hard. Your order is good for the company—easy. Your refunds, rebates, complaints into customer service eat into the bottom line—hard. I'm not sharing this to piss you off; just for you to realize the inherent apathy in most of your relationships with the companies you do business with.

Brands all have "personalities" online now—some are sassy, irreverent, and downright sweet. Ironically, one of the best brands on social media is Wayfair. Yes, many brands now sound like your best friends. They purport to care about you as an individual, even use slang, but beneath the veneer of friendship is their real goal—revenue and profit growth above all else.

ANYTHING YOU SAY ON THIS CALL CAN AND WILL BE USED AGAINST YOU

Calling customer service is like calling your crooked cousin, who is definitely wearing a wire. You keep thinking to yourself, "no one talks like this." Only people being recorded say, "I want to make sure you would agree I took care of everything to fix your account, and I was very helpful to you." Unless you're friends with Zuckerberg, do you know anyone in your real life who says, "I do apologize for that"? Then becomes your fake best friend. "I see you've been a loyal customer for 10 years, great job!"

They talk this way because they've been hired by a department that doesn't trust them to be human. They train the humanity out of the employees and replace it with soviet style conformity that is weird and off-putting most of the time. When you do get a human being to interact with you, they're stripped of all humanity. It's worse than a chat with Amazon's Alexa. This is why we've gotten used to "Did you find everything OK?" from every cashier. Next time respond with "No." The conversation ends there; the question is rhetorical. You're not talking to a human being. The customer service department the cashier works for forces them to leave their humanity at the door. Organic humanity doesn't scale well and is replaced with artificial humanity—a trained fake niceness. It's akin to spending a night in a cheap hotel—it's a room with a bed but will never be a bedroom. Even when they don't resolve your issue, they still ask, "Is there anything else I can do for you?" If it feels like performance art—it is.

THE LIES START EARLY AND OFTEN

Our generation spends about 43 days of our lives on hold. We spend double that time waiting in person and on-line for someone to respond. The wait is only getting longer. Executive after executive at your favorite brand promises to "improve the customer experience" only to add technology you didn't ask for to customer service. Sometimes it's not all bad. It's not what you asked for but will maybe mollify you. Most times, it makes things worse.

How come every insurance company has an ad stating they're cheaper than their competition? It is impossible for that to be true, it's no wonder why, like every other institution, we no longer trust companies. The promises just get grander, raising the customers' expectations, but in the end, Customer Service is getting fewer investments per customer. The lies start as soon as you have a problem and need customer service. You call a 1-800 #, and it starts with "please listen carefully, our menu has recently changed." It hasn't. "We will be with you shortly." They won't. "Your call is very important to us." It isn't. If it was important to them, they'd be talking to you right now. "Your call will be answered in the order it was received" is also a lie. There's a logic that gives priority to different people. Even the sacred "Your call may be recorded for quality and training purposes" now sounds sarcastic. What training and what quality are you receiving in exchange for passive consent to your call being recorded? It's being recorded for their benefit, not ours.

The teller at the checkout line tells you to give her your email to send you a receipt. Before long, you have 50 emails with coupons you don't need, and now you need to click a tiny text at the bottom of the email to make it stop. The lies are early and often. It's time we have an honest relationship, one where the gap between expectations and reality is reduced.

HAS ALL TRUST WITH SERVICE ERODED?

Imagine being deployed and coming home to a refund check from your insurance company. During the war, USAA will refund premiums to military families for the dates they were deployed without solicitation. USAA knows they couldn't justify charging you a premium while you were away defending our country. Many of those families will refuse the refunds. USAA will insist they keep them. Contrast that with my Internet service provider when my internet was out for three weeks. AT&T knew about it but didn't give me credit. The only way I would get any credit is to call them, wait for an hour, go through interrogation, and maybe I'll get a credit.

The reason every relationship fails is unmet expectations. The thing is, as customers, we can't help but have expectations because of the endless promises. The promises start at the point of purchase, commercials that ultimately lead to disappointment, followed by more promises, and the cycle continues.

Even your privacy and safety isn't sacred. People break into your home, pick up your phone, and start paying your bills. This happens often; really, it does! At least that's what my bank thinks. Why else do I go through an interrogation to pay a bill. We're all used to having to answer some interrogation questions before being allowed to receive service. If you've been paying attention to the news, you must know that hackers seem to be outgunning the biggest corporations on the planet. These questions about your mother's maiden name aren't keeping you and me safe.

Think about it. How hard is it for anyone to figure out your mother's maiden name or your childhood street? Anyone with a little determination and a slow internet connection can crack that code. So if it is not keeping us safe, why does it persist? Well, it still serves two purposes. It adds a barrier between you and the service, buying the company some time for "their systems to load." Even if it isn't completely useless and still provides a thin layer of protection. It's like TSA screening. They let in guns 80% of the time, but we should be thankful it works 20% the time? I guess it is slightly better than doing nothing.

There are things both effective and not annoying they can do but choose not to. For example, more companies are using ownership authentication, voice bios, or even two-factor authentication. The companies using those for service do so because they have to, so it tends to be your financial institution. Even though the stakes may be higher with some other organizations, they're waiting for costs to come down or regulation to force them to comply.

What should you do? Make sure to secure all your accounts and practice better consumer hygiene with passwords. Take advantage of additional security layers they provide, like two-factor authentication. Take your security into your own hands when you reach out for service. If you find that it's too easy to access your accounts, find a different company that takes security more seriously.

CUSTOMER SERVICE FAILS SERVICE WORKERS EVEN MORE

The only thing worse than calling customer service is working in customer service. The bigger the company, the worse that job might be. Let's start with those who work in call or contact centers. This is not where the company invests heavily. The idea is to spend enough on customer service to mollify you but not satisfy you.

Federal prisoners have more freedom than call center agents

They measure everything—I mean everything, including bathroom breaks and how long they last. It's been 20 years, and I still remember my days on the front line. As a call center agent, my boss would show me weekly reports of how long my bathroom breaks lasted. I'd also be informed of the number of times I put a customer on hold and how long my calls were. Then I was instructed to listen to a recording of the worst call I had that week. Every CEO talks about the importance of taking care of the customer. Yet, time after time, they hire people they don't trust and then put them in charge of making customers happy.

One spring morning a decade ago, I had two teary-eyed employees in my office. One was an excellent frontline customer service rep, and the other was her manager. I couldn't make out much of what she was saying but heard enough to understand a customer called her a F'ing B*$%! I did my best to console them and assured them I was on the case. Within minutes, I was listening to the recordings from the interactions—there was no polishing this turd. This was a bad call. She was a saint, but the customer was relentless. Let's just say my already expansive profanity dictionary expanded by a few words. Apparently, there were six similar unreported calls from this customer that were just as inflammatory. I reached out to my bosses and requested a rubber stamp to end this customer relationship. They looked over the customer profile. It turned out he was a big account.

With the almighty dollar guiding our thinking, we took a left turn on rationalization street. We had come to the cowardly conclusion that occasional customer abuse was par for the course, and a little yelling sprinkled with mild profanity was fine for all customer service employees. We did, however, use financial compensation to draw that line. We concluded that we didn't pay our frontline employees enough to be called a F$%&ing B&$#! So we established that those calls should be immediately sent on to the supervisors and managers (they were paid more). So, just like that, we had a new policy for handling abusive customers—we paid supervisors more, they could handle it.

It's common for senior leaders to patronize people in customer service by saying they have "hard jobs that are invaluable" but then do little to better their overall experience. I was a terrible advocate for those ladies. I folded like a cheap lawn chair as soon as I got pushback. I chose not to buck the system—I was worried about my interests instead of standing up for them.

I've worked with 100 companies over the years and can tell you that even companies with God-awful technologies for their call center somehow manage to first invest in a high functioning website to attract new customers. Meanwhile, the customer service rep has 50 green screen windows open with little insight into what the customer called about 10 minutes ago. The 'Solution': every customer service agent gets two monitors!

I attended an all-employee meeting at one of the largest retailers in America. The CEO and other team members paid homage to customer service by saying, "You are the people with the most difficult jobs in the company," and "We can't do it without you." The service people don't want to be heroes. Recognition is nice but functioning tools, better pay, and to stop telling them when they can use the restroom are far better than an empty compliment.

Maybe the most scandalous part of this is the pay. Customer Service employees are one of the lowest-paid at most companies, yet everyone admits that if the marketing staff stops showing up to work, it will suck for a while, but ultimately, the company keeps moving. If everyone in Customer Service stops showing up, the company will grind to a halt and end up being investigated. If you're reading this and have the power or influence to make changes, please do so. Service employees don't want to be heroes, but If they are heroes as you keep insisting, they need to be paid like Tony Stark or even Batman.

EMPLOYEE FIRST, CUSTOMER SECOND

I asked an executive friend if he would let his 20-year-old son work in his customer service department. He looked at me as if I asked if his son could join ISIS. This view of the CS profession has to change radically, not because of some intangible reason but because without that change, zero service is not possible.

If you happen to be a leader responsible for service, please pay attention. I have no doubt you have asked a lot from these employees, but for once, let them do the asking. It's your turn to serve them. Ask them how you can be helpful, and you will get a laundry list of requests. Let's review what may be on that list.

I suspect that list will include compensation. You can laud their efforts to the heavens, but it'll fall on deaf ears if you're not trying to get them adequately compensated. This is no easy task. You won't be getting a standing ovation when you go to your CFO asking for more money to invest in the frontline, especially if the organization views customer service as an assembly line. This is where you come in—you are the one to make the case.

They're also going to ask you for your trust, for you to loosen the reins a little. Perhaps eliminate the checklists and everything that screams, "I don't trust you or your decision making." This includes overly prescriptive policies and metrics like Average Handle Time that give you a false sense of control but hurt the customer experience.

    Lastly, there will be many items about the customer—their customer. No one can better articulate the problem with your customer experience than your frontline. It's going to be painful for you to hear, but you need to hear all of it to help you prioritize where to start. Hopefully, this book will give you ideas on how you might tackle them. Readying for the next era of service requires that you have the right people—empowered people. The stakes are high on the journey of improving your customer experience. You should stop saying, "Our representatives are the most important people in the company," when your actions say otherwise. Empty words make things worse. Focus on finding ways you can empower them to be effective on the frontline. Live the principle of employee first, customer second.

Before Technology came to kill us

THOSE ANNOYING CHATBOTS

If chatbots feel familiarly painful, it's because they're not new. It's the same crappy automated phone system you hate, now brought to life in text form. Chatbots have a 75% failure rate. I did a podcast episode arguing whether we should abandon this idea altogether. I predicted the failure of chatbots years before they became prevalent. It wasn't a hard prediction to make. The primary uses of chatbots are customer service-related.

Chatbots measure everything through the prism of providing customer service for as little as possible. What you want is a tool that does the job well or transfers you to a real human when it can't resolve the issue. What most organizations ask us to do is take their automated phone system and create a text version. Chatbots feel familiar because it's the same crappy automated phone system you despise, brought to life in text form.

Customer Service isn't about making you happy. It's about making you less mad at the cheapest price. I was on a Zoom call with the CTO of a government agency. He wanted me to give him a quote to build him a chatbot. I asked him my standard question: "Do you want a bad bot or a good bot?"

He hemmed for a moment. "Of course, I want the good bot."

I asked more questions. He ended up asking me to build something about halfway between a good bot and a bad bot. It's not just the technology that makes or breaks it; it's also how much time and resources the organization is willing to invest in making sure the bot can understand, empathize, and resolve your issue.

As technological developments like Natural Language Processing and Machine Learning become more prevalent, we finally have a machine that can handle customer service inquiries on its own. None of it happens magically. You have to treat the bot like a toddler, train it, correct it when it gets something wrong, and make it smarter by feeding it vast amounts of data, or you can pay a lot of money to buy a teenage bot, one trained by someone else. In either case, it's a commitment, and because Customer Service teams are generally treated as a necessary evil, most companies don't get this right, ergo the 75% failure rate.

How to avoid chatbot pain

Great bots are available. I'm proud of two I built for major brands. Odds are you'll be interacting with a bad bot since most of them are designed that way. When you do, breathe deeply, you'll need patience. There are two ways to play this. One is to avoid the bot at all costs by asking for a representative over and over till it transfers you. Just like the phone system, buckle up. It'll take a while, and the bot, like the phone system, may be programmed to not transfer you.

A second approach is to lean in. Automation is not the enemy. Automation can produce a superior experience to a human for specific issues. If all you need is a $20 withdrawal, the best option is an ATM. That experience is superior to the bank teller. Ask yourself: is your task the equivalent of a $20 withdrawal? If so, engage with the bot, but if your task is more complex, avoid the bot and head over to their social media page or the dreaded telephone. If that fails, go to the section where we offer tools for you to navigate the labyrinth.

TECHNOLOGY HAS THE WHEEL

Let me first defend technology before coming for it's head. Technology is an extension of ourselves. Centuries ago, some of the hottest pieces of technology were silverware, then it was the car, then the airplane. As soon as the technology becomes useful, it stops being called technology and is assigned a friendlier name. The focus of service is about how to mollify customers at the cheapest possible cost. Technology is good at driving costs down, but technology that goes beyond mollification requires a lot more thought, energy, and money. The result is that we've been conducting a live experiment on customer service since the 90s that has no end in sight. Service organizations are under cost pressure. The company makes it clear there is no ROI in hiring people to resolve your issues but is willing to spend on technology so long as it eliminates the need for more people. This is how we ended up at this moment. Allow me a trip down memory lane.

Imagine what customer service was like before we could make cheap phone calls at scale. Then imagine if American Airlines canceled a flight, and all passengers had to physically show up at their office. Enter the 20th century when we invented the technology that allowed us to call companies at scale from anywhere in the world. Thus began the formalization of the customer service & call center professions. Over time, there was more and more need to call customer service, so the companies got tired of spending money. Technology promised to help the companies speak to more and more people at a cheaper and cheaper rate.

I CAN'T CALL A 1-800 # IN FRONT OF YOUNG CHILDREN

The automated phone system started as a simple press 1, press 2 to help the company send you to the right department. The first iteration was superior to the human. We replaced the person playing air traffic control—deciding who answered the call and manually transferring everyone by hand. The natural progression was "what if you could call anytime and instead of talking to a person, the machine gave you the answer." This started small; questions like "what are your store hours?" were placed on the phone system accessible without needing to pay anyone to talk to you. We then decided to automate more complex inquiries to mixed results and mostly disastrous results. Before you know it, your press 1 or 2 became a multi-layered menu too confusing to be useful. Customers started trying to opt out. Instead of viewing that as a sign to simplify, to only use this technology for few scenarios with a high degree of success, the opposite happened. Automation is a blunt instrument for cash-starved service departments, so they pressed on.

How did service departments react to consumers wanting out of the automated systems they hated? Did they sit down with you and figure out why you hate the confusing menu tree? Nope. They doubled down, making it near impossible for you to ever opt out. In one year alone, we were hired to make sure you can't speak to a human without at least trying to figure out the maze of options at least 4 different times. I have been trapped many times in what I've dubbed "IVR jail." As we speak, your favorite companies are still adding voice responses, so you may find yourself cursing out the bot like I often do. Your call is considered "low value," the work you entrust to a poorly built automated system. If your call was high value (will produce income), the last thing they want is to frustrate you.

What did the industry learn from 30 years of putting ill-fated technology between you and the help you need? It learned that it could get away with it. Haven't you caved in and eventually tried to deal with the machine? We all have. The feedback that it sends to Customer Service leadership is that it works. An executive at a communications company client proudly told me, "Our IVR handles 24 Million calls a year. That's an annual savings of $50M." I called this IVR, and it was awful and impossible to escape. His customers were holding their noses and dealing with it. What he called 'success' in customer service was giving you just enough service. Good luck getting him to invest in the system or people. As he saw it, no matter what I told him about the terrible system, he just cared about the bottom line and asked me to justify why he should spend more improving the system for you. I suggested that if he treated you better, you'd refer his business to your friends and remain a loyal customer. He nodded in agreement but deep down, he never believed you'd leave. And most times, he was right. His service sucked because we let him get away with it.

People like me (consultants) are responsible for most of what customer experience looks like. It doesn't matter what company you do business with. Once they get to a certain size, they all end up doing similar things. They do so because everything I implement at the biggest companies then gets copied and pasted to all other companies. Then people like me also decide what is "best practice," then publish it—a reinforcing loop of conformity and why every company's 1800# lies about "our menu options have changed" in the same monotone voice.

CONSULTANTS HAVE SOLD OUT TO BIG TECHNOLOGY COMPANIES

Let me bring you behind the curtain to help you understand how the echo chamber works. Imagine you're the executive responsible for customer service at one of the biggest corporations in the world. You want to make a difference, so you can get a big bonus and move to an even bigger office. The problem is, you don't know the first thing about customer service, so you need some help. From what you learned from business school, you seek out the "experts." The problem is all the experts want to do is sell you technology, and even when they don't sell technology, they "implement" technology. That's where all the money and energy goes, so even when all you need is to change the schedule of the people you have, there is always technology being sold to you.

When I started 20 years ago, there was a bright line between experts who would give you advice and technology companies. The advisory companies shared the know-how—empowering your employees to do the right thing, setting up your process and technology so it's friendly. The technology company wanted to sell you software and hardware, and you could trust the advisory company to be agnostic and just call balls and strikes. The technology company realized that not only was there serious cash in technology but that the only people standing in their way were the "advice" people—people like me who wanted to "think things through." So before long, all the firms who gave advice got in bed with the technology companies—by force (acquisition), by greed (cooperation), and reluctantly 'coopetition'.

Now everyone advising your favorite brands to improve your service is saying one thing and one thing only—use technology. Worse than that, the technology firms set the agenda and create the buzzwords of what is trendy. The hot thing is always coded in words that sound flowery but are ultimately about the next technology that will save the company money and improve your experience.

From 2009-2015, they convinced us that the one thing customers wanted was OmniChannel. You never asked for OmniChannel or even knew what the heck that meant. Yet, for years, we were told by experts that the number one problem customers have was the ability to start a transaction on a website, then pick up that same conversation on the phone, then pick it up again in store. Of course, it never worked, and no one asked for it, but It didn't stop the industry from pouring billions of dollars into this doomed idea. There have been many more, but this feedback loop is dangerous and makes me bearish on customer service. If the technology companies, well-meaning and all, have unchallenged control of what customer service is or isn't.

I've said so many bad things about technology that you might think I'm a technophobe. Au contraire, I'm a technophile; I have had a smart home before most people knew what that meant. I got into the customer service industry as a developer. I'm an unabashed, recovering technologist. I just happen to be a humanist first. I'm proud of some of the technology solutions I've designed and implemented. They all have one thing in common—the technology solution is usually superior to dealing with a human. That's a high bar, but it should be higher.

How do you know if technology has crossed this bar? You'll pick the technology over a human every time. If I want to check my account balance, the app is vastly superior to talking to a human. Technology has also democratized customer service at scale. There are plenty of companies who couldn't even provide mediocre service at any scale without the power of technology. What we need is balance, back to a place where there is more than one voice in the room. We agree to use technology where it makes sense and in ways that objectively improve the experience.

MRS. LINCOLN, OTHER THAN THAT, HOW DID YOU ENJOY THE PLAY?

After spending most of my day in an airport because my friends at Delta airlines thought I needed a 3-hour delay so I could enjoy some airport sushi, I got a survey. They wanted my feedback! Here's a disturbing new trend—machines in airport bathrooms that you're supposed to touch AFTER using the bathroom to indicate whether or not you were satisfied with your bathroom experience. This is the natural escalation of things; we're being surveyed every time we do anything. I can't go to any website without someone wanting me to take a survey. After every call, email, purchase, there's a survey. We're all survey fatigued, but that isn't even the bad part.

Are company representatives better at meeting customer expectations because of these surveys? What improvements to the customer experience are happening because of this feedback?

Let's start with what happens with all the surveys. While they send the survey to you, no one cares about your feedback. What the company cares about is a number. An aggregated survey score is primarily used for marketing purposes, secondarily for executive incentives, and if your response is extremely negative, you might get some attention. There's a cottage industry led by big tech companies—the story goes something like this: there's a magic score that if customers give you good feedback, good things will happen. By good things, they mean you'll likely buy more stuff. This is shaky math. Human beings don't work this way. The fact that I had a good rating today because the McDonald's drive-through worked like it should doesn't mean I'm now a McDonald's fanboy.

When I was a customer service executive, a big part of my bonus was tied to something called a Net promoter Score*. It is a survey that asks how likely you are to recommend a product or service. Since my bonus and the bonus of all executives were tied to this number, we had one mission—make sure the number goes up. Some think this is a good thing for customer service, but they're wrong. Because when it becomes about a number, there are a thousand ways to get the number to move without making a lasting positive change to customer service. Companies like J.D Power, Gallup, and their ilk who track customer satisfaction scores show some improvement in customer satisfaction scores. Most of these 'satisfaction scores' have to do with incentive structures designed to improve these scores. It's a racket. The underlying experience hasn't improved.

Does your survey get rolled up into a score only so executives get bonuses? Not exactly. Your scores are also used to punish, so while executives get big bonuses, customer service gets harshly punished if you give a low score. If you check the box requesting a callback, your survey will be flagged as a squeaky wheel, and you might get some attention. What about the comments and paragraphs you wrote hoping a human will read? That ends up in an entity called a 'word cloud' and fed into AI to aggregate and come up with a summary.

Remember the recording we hear every time we call customer service—"your call may be recorded for quality and training purposes." Half that statement is true; most of the calls are recorded. It's not for quality and training so much as it's weaponized against the customer service agent. Recording is another opportunity to assign a numerical value to your customer service experience. Most companies don't assign the manpower to listen to enough samples to be meaningful. The practice does more harm than good from a customer experience perspective. Imagine if your calls are recorded and used against you—this is the reality of customer service representatives. They're punished if they forget to "use your name," forget to remind you of a promotion, or any number of petty grievances. To be fair, they're also used for compliance and legal reasons, but as far as improving the quality of your experience, they're fairly useless.

There's still value in taking the surveys. That poor customer service associate can get rewarded for doing a good job. They're underpaid and overworked, so to the extent you have an opportunity to tell the world they did a good job, please do. The survey isn't the best medium to express frustration. You can put your issues in the comments, but often time it's a third party that conducts the survey, and if your data is anonymized, they may not even be able to get you help.

My book is focused on defining the problems with customer service, but I'll point out that some organizations do a decent job with feedback. The key differentiation for them has to do with follow-through. These organizations are respectful of your time and do two things well. They do follow up with customers who request follow-ups, and they do try to use the data to improve the experience within the limits of customer mollification. These organizations have tackled the painfully obvious customer service issues; they now truly want feedback to improve. If the company you're dealing with can't answer the phone on time, stop responding to their feedback. They already know their problems; more feedback won't help.

Most Customer service issues are painfully obvious to the company you're interacting with. They don't need your survey to find out how long you waited in line. Asking you if you were satisfied with the service when they know the service was terrible is pouring salt on an open wound. It's like they're not trying to use the data.

When I contact my insurance company, the 800# verifies the number I'm calling from and asks if it's the number on my account. I answer in the affirmative. It then asks me why I might be calling, and I say, "customer service."

It then insists I need to be more specific and provides me a list of options to choose from. I oblige only to be asked what service I have with them (I only had one).

They could use data to better predict what I want, and it comes with the byproduct of automatically creating a better customer service experience.

Suppose that the same IVR (automated phone system) was designed so that once it identified my phone number and then pulled up my account, it now knows what service I have, and the options are narrowed. Already we'd have progress. They could take a step further, given that they have all this data about me, and safely predict why I'm calling. If you combine the data, it's how clairvoyant they can be.

I remember setting out 11 years ago to accurately predict why our online retail consumers would be calling, and I put a target of 65%. We ended up exceeding that goal. We were internally complex, but once we took an outside-in view, we realized our consumers saw their reasons for calling in simple terms. Once we mirrored their thinking, we broke all inquiries down into two simplistic blocks. Then, by utilizing more data points, we could get more specific. For example: if we knew the customer's order status, time of day, and expected delivery date, we could predict with a high degree of certainty why the customer might be calling.

This is real progress, but there's another step they can take fairly easily. They can send all information in a simple format using CTI (computer telephony integration) technology that's been available for 20 years—they pass on the data collected, so the service rep knows why they're contacting you. Then my phone call to any company can be, "Hello Amas, it looks like you are having some trouble with your delivery. I already found out what the issue is. We will deliver tomorrow morning.

I have raised the issue with the supply chain department and will follow up with my teammates in the next two days to ensure it doesn't happen again. I will send you my findings."

This is an experience that shifts the hard work from customers and underpaid employees to data-driven technology that removes friction conversation with your customers.

OUTSOURCING OVERSEAS

My flight landed in Bogota. We were picked up by a nice young man who held a sign with my name on it. That had never happened to me before, so for a 20-something, it felt being royalty. I was escorted by two men who took me to a black SUV with two men holding AK 47s. I became concerned but kept my cool. Riding in the SUV, I rolled down the window to take in the city. The driver and my handler spoke in Spanish. I was then requested to put my hands in the vehicle and roll up the window. He said matter-of-fact, "Those men riding motorbikes are prepared to cut off your wrist to get their hands on your gold plated watch."

Why was I in Colombia risking my life? To find cancer-saving drugs? No, to find cheaper labor to deliver customer service. For American companies, the most expensive part of customer service is to pay someone to talk to you. To avoid that, they look for ways to not talk to you at all. If that fails, it becomes finding you the cheapest possible person to talk to you. Paying a customer service worker a low wage isn't low enough, so the next best thing is a whole world away.

This practice of matching customers with service from people they can't understand was initiated in the 90s and accelerated in the 2000s. Back then, I'd developed software I was trying to sell. My product performed many functions, but the best thing it did was accent neutralization. I was confident it was going to be BIG. We were in the early stages of outsourcing customer service. The first set of English-speaking cities America outsourced its calls to were in India. While their English was good, the accent was a non-starter for most Americans. It was painful for customers.

I've yet to meet one person who's a fan 25 years later, and yet outsourcing is ever more popular. Why does it persist? Money.

As recently as 2014, a big part of my job was about traveling the world in search of the cheapest labor I could find to handle customer service at the cheapest cost. I went to Africa, Southeast Asia, Latin America, even countries you didn't know existed. It hasn't been all bad; we even went to a lovely country called Guyana, a paradise, all to save a dollar in customer service.

The cost-saving pressures in Customer Service are such that even when you know what you're doing is frustrating customers, it still feels like an option if you see customer service as a necessary evil. You treat it the way my teenage son treats cleaning his room—you do just enough.

WHAT CUSTOMER SUCCESS CAN TEACH US ABOUT CUSTOMER SERVICE

There's a well-functioning corner of the border customer service aptly called customer success. If I were writing a book focused on this corner of service, I'd have a lot fewer things to complain about. If you're a customer service professional reading this, get to know customer success. Customer success teams focus less on customer mollification and instead on customer utilization. They're focused on not just "resolving" customer issues but also getting the customer to get the most utility from the goods and services they're purchasing. They want you to buy more stuff by helping you utilize your outcomes from what you already bought.

The financial incentives for both the company and customers are aligned in the way it isn't for most of customer service. Why are they so aligned? For most customer service organizations, the money spent on customer service impacts the bottom line negatively. In customer success, money well spent on customer service impacts the top and bottom line positively. The industry that popularized this profession is software sales in general and in particular SaaS companies—Software as a Service. For these companies, you pay by the drink, if you will. They charge you a monthly rate to use their service. If you decide it isn't working the following month, you can walk away and hire another company. The happier you are with the modules you're using, the more services they can sell you.

With this economic model, it makes sense to put as many resources as possible into customer service—or, as they call it, customer success because there's a direct line to revenue and profit. There is more to learn from customer success because the model of service is also counter to most service organizations.

They seek out problems before they happen. They're well-resourced to handle the obvious and reactive service but also play offense. They try to be proactive about service. Last week my internet service was out due to an outage in my neighborhood. It was back on in 24 hours. I never heard a word from them during the outage or after. I got most of my neighbor's updates on the NextDoor social media app. I suspect that if my utilization of their service was financially important to them, I would've been notified and apprised every step of the way. My outage is their outage; my dissatisfaction doesn't just make them sad, it hurts them financially. As we think about a way forward, the alignment of goals is a key leg of the stool for the future of customer service

The Future of Service

THE WAY FORWARD

Prosecution's closing argument against Customer Service

The profession of customer service is charged with several counts, with the most serious 3 charges being:

Count I. Lack of customer access – Customers experience increasingly long waits, lack of access to the channel of their choice, or no access at all to service when they need it.

Count II- High customer effort - Customers are being asked to do a lot more work to get service. Examples include having to call to check on the status of a delivery when the company should do all the work.

Count III- Unfair treatment of customers - Rude and inconsiderate service as well as downright selfish policies.

On Count I

Every company has a customer access strategy, whether official or unofficial. Some are well thought out, but most of them were arrived at by accident. The customer access strategy defines your access to their customer service. The first thing most companies decide is how they prefer to interact with you. They make conscious decisions regarding the following options.

First: Channels. How they deliver the service to you, be it in person, mail, telephone, email, chat, social media, video, and so on. The best run service companies would, with help from someone like me, start mapping these channels to the issues that make sense. For example: it makes more sense for you to do technical troubleshooting over chat or phone as opposed to email. Next comes determining hours of operations. 24/7 would be nice, but it's expensive and sometimes unnecessary. Finding the middle ground between 24/7 and only a few hours a day is a bit of art and a bit of science. What most companies resort to is make the channels that cost them nothing, like the websites, available all the times and the expensive channels available a certain amount of time.

Second is how quickly to respond to your inquiry. There are several ways these are set. In essence, they want to count how long it took you from the moment the phone started ringing (or when you walked in) till the point you got your issue handled. Most companies have a target of 30 seconds to answer the phone, so they might have a goal of 90% service level. If 90% of people are in and out in 30 seconds, then it is a success. Setting this goal and meeting this goal comes down to resources—do they have enough people at the right times for the goal to be met?

The next sets of decisions involve tools—how much technology to put between you and your request and how much pain you're willing to tolerate. Most companies don't take a comprehensive approach and can't articulate how much or how little technology customers have to endure or enjoy. We were doing work for a bank many years ago, and I created a challenge of sorts, a bit like a treasure hunt. I asked their executives to call their 1800# and complete a set of challenges like to call and speak to a representative. They came back mortified, and the CEO said, "I'd rather get waterboarded than talk to that stupid machine." They have one of the most customer-friendly phone systems today.

Next is planning and forecasting. Based on the access strategy, most companies begin to forecast and plan. Based on how many units they sold, they can use historical data or other assumptions to predict how many times someone will need to speak to customer service. They then implement staffing and scheduling, and where much of the pain customers experience starts. Instead of staffing and scheduling based on the need, they staff and schedule based on the "budget." That's inherently bad by design. On the count of customer access, not only are organizations guilty as charged, this is a case of willful disregard of the implicit and explicit brand promises made.

On Count II

We have to examine the many ways customer service puts the burden on you, the customer, and whether we can find fault with the companies we do business with. This has been slowly gaining steam and is now at a crescendo. As companies tried to save cost on labor, they've shifted the burden to two options—machines and customers.

Consider your grocery shopping experience. I'm not that old, but in my lifetime, we used to have help storewide while you shop, culminating in someone bagging your groceries and bringing them to your car. Today you may have to climb a ladder to get your groceries, bag them yourself, use a wand to scan and pay, then carry the bags to your car.

The digital experience isn't any better. You go online, and before anyone will help you, you have to fill out forms and re-enter information in multiple places. God forbid you call a phone number. There are never-ending menu options designed to force you to talk to a machine. If you get through, then inevitably, the employee asks you to repeat every piece of information you thought you just shared. Pray that you don't get transferred or the call drops. You have to start all over again.

Every time the system they built fails you, you get an apology that sounds like, "I know you already provided it, but unfortunately, the system didn't transfer your information. Can I get the last 4 of your social and your zip code again?"

This might be one of the easiest parts of customer service to fix. In part because it's not as expensive or complicated to fix. Let's take a vexing problem we all have—the lack of proactivity from customer service teams. Why are you the one checking on the status of your issue? Why are you the one figuring out and telling the company that your delivery is late? They have much more information than you do and should be contacting you.

Consider the idiotic question we all get at the end of talking to anyone in customer service: "Is there anything else I can help you with?" This question sounds good on the surface until you realize the person who knows the answer is the person answering it. Only the company employees know what else is wrong or what else you might need from customer service. Let's say you were on chat with your gas company and want to change your due date. You got the assistance you needed, and they then asked, "what else can I help you with?" A better path forward would be to say, "I have completed your due date change. Would you like me to show you what your next bill will look like since it will be prorated?" Instead of asking the customer to do the work, it will cost nothing to anticipate the next need.

On Count III

How about the policies and procedures that are so customer unfriendly? Is it all random? Have you just been unlucky?

Let's review some of the most common complaints. It starts at the point of purchase. When they sell you the goods and services, promises are made explicitly and implicitly that you can reach customer service and your issue will be resolved.

In many cases, the reason you bought the product or service was in part due to the positive claims about Customer Service. Then you find out they prefer not to hear from you by making communications difficult. I've lately been dealing with problems with my cell service in silence because for me to even think of contacting service, the problem needs to be a lot more serious.

Is this intentional? Well, every organization has to make decisions around policies and procedures, and the rule of thumb for most service organizations is to manage to the exception. Nordstrom has a one-sentence employee handbook that says, "We'll do what we believe to be best for our business and our employee community." Service organizations are cost-conscious and have not met a policy they didn't like. Imagine how humorless the IRS rulebook is. That is how most customer service organizations think. They assume that most customers who contact CS have nothing better to do than try to rip off the company they do business with. Thus customer service organizations manage by exceptions.

Let's take my example of a large furniture retailer I recently did business with. I bought a hot tub in early 2021 and just kept waiting for delivery. I ended up contacting them four months later to cancel the order after they said it wouldn't arrive for several more months. I had to spend 3 hours of my day, including on hold, waiting for a supervisor just so they could do something that's a no-brainer. Why is the policy that if someone wants to cancel an order has to go through hell? So that most people will give up and end up keeping something they don't want. Maybe one customer years ago tried to take advantage of them and so now ALL customers must be punished.

As a former customer service executive, I can tell you these pressure are real. I was measured on a few numbers. First was cost—how much did I spend to make sure customers did not hate us? The lower the number, the higher my bonus. My team was also measured by how many credits we received, which factored into the cost per customer. The only way to make sure these numbers stay low is through draconian policies. I visited a customer service organization that took away the credit button from its frontline staff.

Why won't these companies just be honest and direct with what customer service would look like? Instead of "satisfaction guaranteed or your money back," we got "satisfaction, or you can try to get your money back only if you can jump through hoops." There is short-term thinking everywhere, but in customer service, the motto is, "We already have your money, please don't hate us too much." Would you buy from a more honest company?

IN DEFENSE OF CUSTOMER SERVICE

Is there a defense for the long rap sheet of customer service? I gathered some of the best minds in customer service. I promised them anonymity, and it got real. The first thing that came up was customer expectations. They shared that customer expectations have become unrealistic, that customer service has gotten a lot better, but customer expectations have just risen even higher.

I would say expectations are rising everywhere. My standard expectation now for anything I order is that it arrives in 48 hours, and I can return it without paying a dime. My base expectation is that I can use witchcraft to summon a chariot to pick me up from anywhere in the world, and while being chauffeured, I can order food that will arrive at the same time my car gets there. It's a fair point.

Expectations have risen but has customer service gotten better? I looked at hard evidence and agree that many parts of Customer Service have indeed gotten a lot better. For one thing, customers who like to self-service instead of interacting with another human will testify to things getting better. You can check your balance or track an order while lying in bed. Almost all Customer Service improvements have been centered around new technology. Outside of that, there have been legendary stories like the Zappos customer service person who ordered a customer flowers. These stories outside of self-service are amazing because they're much outside the norm. Customer survey data shows some years were better than others, but overall, the data concludes that only 8% of customers agree things are going well.

I've concluded that a demanding public as a source for what's plaguing CS is a weak defense. Yes, some corners of customer service have improved, and while customer expectations have increased, the core parts of customer service have gotten worse. The more insidious part of this is where do we, as customers, get these expectations from? These expectations are created by the same companies' marketing department that promises "satisfaction guaranteed" and who also keeps you on hold for an hour. The same company that shows a perfect burger made by the gods only, hands you a burger that looks like it's been sat on. Dishonest advertising initiates the gap in what is being promised and delivered. By the time Customer Service steps in, the barn doors are wide open, and the horses have escaped.

This gap can be the source of the solution. We need a new customer service bill of rights or a new social contract. Here are several suggestions.

THREE BOLD IDEAS FOR CUSTOMER SERVICE

Brutally honest expectation setting

The problem with customer service comes down to two words: Unmet Expectations. It's painfully obvious to me, having worked with C-Suite executives for many years, that the vast majority of companies have zero desire to provide the kind of service many customers want. Brutal honesty doesn't get rewarded. It's like our relationship with politicians. We bemoan their lies but rarely vote for the truth-teller. What if a politician in America comes out and says, "Look, we have a spending and revenue problem. Everyone will feel the pinch, including seniors who consume a disproportionate amount of the spending."

If the politician is brutally honest about the state of things and the hard road ahead, they will be a fringe candidate. Instead, the candidates who win pick their spots in being candid but mostly tell us what we want to hear. We vote for them and are shocked at the outcomes.

Like we need brutal honesty from politicians, we need it even more from the companies we interact with. The fact is that companies want to provide the best customer service to their constituents at the lowest possible cost. When there's friction between the best service and cost, the cost usually wins out. This is true for virtually all companies out there. We need to move the conversation from an emotional place and focus on hard facts. Maybe this is why I'm not in marketing or politics. I think and believe that treating humans as adults and being honest is a net positive.

Let's use McDonald's as an example. Here is their current claim about service.

If you are not satisfied, we will make it right—or your next meal is on us.

This is a company with a dollar menu and has the perception of being inexpensive. If we're to examine this claim, it means that every customer who spends $1 on a sandwich is guaranteed to be satisfied. What exactly does satisfied mean? That your stomach will be appeased? Your food will be fast and hot? Let's assume it's subjective. If you have any complaints, McDonald's will make it right.

How exactly will McDonald's "make it right"? The customer spent a few dollars on the meal, and now McDonald's guarantees every customer out there that they're prepared to lose money on every hamburger sold? A publicly-traded company is promising that no matter how much or little you spend, they will "make it right" and/or lose money trying?

Let me put a finer point on it. I was hired to do work by one of the largest fast-food chains in the world. What did they hire me to do? Well, they were spending way too much on customer service. In their case, the average customer spent $6 while costing them $4 every time the phone rang on a complaint. They had thin margins, to begin with, but once you complained, the profit was gone, and they were now losing money. They could not afford to deliver decent customer service, yet they offered outlandish customer satisfaction claims.

The future of honest customer service is one where every organization is clear-eyed about how much it's charging and how much it wants to allocate to customer service. We should see tickers and banners showing how long customers are in line waiting. Honesty is not just sharing the good; it's sharing the bad and ugly as well.

CUSTOMER SERVICE ECONOMICS - PAY FOR SERVICE

I won't defend Spirit airlines, but they have accidentally created a more honest exchange with customers. They won't be winning any customer service awards, but they don't say they want to. They're focused on cost, some may think too aggressively, but it's quite honest. For one thing, they make it clear up front that it is a budget airline; they do not get defensive about the amenities you will have to pay for, and while it may not be for everyone, it is transparent.

Let's do the economics of traditional customer service. The product you bought cost $100. That price includes the cost to make the product, marketing, customer service, and the profit the company wants. Not everyone contacts customer service, but the cost is included in everyone's price. Some companies have tilted the balance. If you call cell phone providers and credit card companies, there's a fee to talk to a person to do things like making a payment.

Is that the best way to go about changing the economics of customer service? No, but it's a good idea executed wrongly. The first step is transparency. Otherwise, it feels like a bait and switch. When I signed up for my Verizon service, I wasn't told about paying to talk to a human to do certain things. What if Verizon instead was first transparent from the beginning. What if they said, "We have a no-frills plan for $50/

month. It's ideal for the person who never talks to customer service, but should you need to, you'll pay by the drink. Or there's an $80/month plan, reach us anytime, anywhere."

The idea of paying for customer service is jarring, yet customers are tired of bad customer service. Organizations have no incentive to eat into their profits and as long as that dynamic is in place we need new thinking. We can learn from the parts of customer service that work like customer success, where the financial incentives of the person seeking customer service and the company providing it are aligned, we will have better outcomes. In this system, customer service can become a profit center, not indirectly but very directly. It should then pay more to its workers and attract a wider talent pool.

CUSTOMER 'SERVICITIZATION'

An idea that is born from the manufacturing industry is worth exploring. In the old days, if you had a farm or a plant, you paid John Deere to buy the equipment and paid a little more for a service contract or warranty in case it broke. Offering customers an opportunity to pay extra at the point of sale is an idea customer service should copy from the Industrial and manufacturing companies. As jolting as this is to the customer psyche, it's an honest relationship.

There is another layer to this. That industry is evolving into a pay-for-outcome model. You pay a monthly rate that guarantees your equipment or plant is operational. The parts and servicing of said parts are no longer your problem.

This idea isn't all that new, but it has legs. Companies in the smart home space are knee-deep in this model. You pay a monthly fee, and they show up with equipment and services bundled in a guarantee of service level. I hope these elements make their way into the mainstream. They have the potential to generate revenue for organizations and provide better outcomes for customers.

GETTING AROUND CUSTOMER SERVICE

Until customer service is reformed, there are ways to make the rigged game work for you. Let's review the common issues.

Wait times

If you're waiting in line for customer service in person or virtually, there's always a shorter line, even if it isn't the perfect medium for your issue. For example: if you're in a long line at the counter waiting to re-book your flight, while standing in the physical line, call the 1800# while you're waiting, and then while on hold, hop over to Twitter. If you insist on using the phone, many companies now offer an opportunity to call you back and "hold your place in line." The 'hold your place in line' part isn't always true but taking the option allows you to go about your life until it's your turn.

Another trick is for you to pick the option for sales even if you have a service issue. Every company prioritizes the sales line. They figure they already have your money, and all your call is doing is costing them money. On the other hand, there's a new customer who wants to be separated from their wallet. Pick the option that says for sales, and miraculously, your wait will disappear or be a lot shorter.

Shop for the answer you want

Suppose you do talk to someone, and they don't give you an answer you want. Simply hang up and call again. You might get someone else who will give you the answer you want. If that fails, you can escalate the call. Asking for a supervisor is just the start. There are times to bring out bigger guns.

Several years ago, a family friend lost her husband, and he had a medical machine that needed to be returned. His wife neglected to return it in time, and her account was put on a list that resulted in her getting daily phone calls asking to speak to her dead husband. She would get upset and explain her situation again, only for someone else to call the next day. This pattern went on for months. Her son, knowing what I do for a living, asked if I could help. I resolved the issue in 30 minutes. I emailed the company CEO, and the problem went away, and they sent the grieving widow a note of apology.

There are companies devoted to helping you navigate customer service horror stories. One useful tool they have is the ability to get you the contact information of top executives at the company. Bookmark the links we provide in the later pages and use them to your advantage. You won't be speaking to one of these executives. They never get on the phone. Still, they will forward your email or voicemail and tell a subordinate to make you go away. That person will quickly reach out, and because your problem is now the executive's headache, you'll be dealing with a very reasonable person who will find it in their hearts to see reason.

Social Media and old media as a weapon

One powerful tool you have is social media. Although waning, these companies still have some shame left in them. The best way to be successful is to come to social media with proof—a recording, video, picture, and then tweet not only at the company but its executives as well. This is becoming a popular tactic, so many of these companies now have customer service teams on social media, but because it's so public, you do end up getting better service than other channels.

An underutilized medium is snail mail. I probably just lost all readers under 35, but hear me out. No one uses snail mail anymore, so for most companies, almost every piece of snail mail gets looked at thoroughly and tends to be important. If your issue is vexing enough as you type your message in Facebook messenger, email, or whatever tool you are using, simply print a copy of the same message and send copies to all the executives. In many cases, you might be starting a chain that will change that part of the service for the better for you and other customers.

I can't stress this enough: most customer service employees are on your side or neutral. Please don't antagonize them, not only because it's the right thing to do, but because it will make you less effective. Be polite but firm on what you need.

In other cases, you might need to bring one of the 3 or 4 letter agencies into the mix; the newly formed consumer protection bureau can be a good resource. These agencies don't move fast. They're the last resort when you think the company behavior is moving into deceptive or even criminal.

GOVERNMENT AGENCIES WORKAROUND

I've covered the work regarding governmental agencies earlier, but I want to reiterate a couple of things. The most powerful voices are usually not in the room where you're requesting services. They're in old government buildings doing what politicians do. So your strategy if you are not getting help is all about getting past the lines of defense to get to the Queen or King. Sadly, they focus on making the politicians look good versus you getting services, but that is your opportunity. Your job is to align what is good for you with what is good for the politician. Find the political appointee head of the agency's contact information and the appropriate member of congress. Contacting both individuals will get you to the top of the list.

Where do we go from Here?

What I have tried to do in the preceding pages is tell the truth about customer service. I know some of it is uncomfortable to read. I have been part of the problem. My colleagues and I have gotten too clever. Companies have been condescending to customers. What you deserve is the truth. The hard truth. The truth is great human based customer service means lower profits in the short run for shareholders. Instead, consultants like me have done verbal and technical gymnastics to produce customer service that is full of synthetic technology and half-baked processes that leaves everyone unsatisfied. This book may not cause an immediate revolution, in fact many will work hard to discredit it, I am not worried. You do not have to believe a word in this book. I don't believe anyone; I like hard evidence. I am simply telling you the sky is blue and all you must do is simply look out the window for yourself. I have taken the liberty of building a site that will help you and others learn more about customer service and help you navigate difficult world of customer service, simply scan the bar code on the following pages or visit waitingforservice.com

Join the Revolution.

Scan the Bar Code to learn how to avoid Terrible Service

WAITING FOR SERVICE

[QR Code - SCAN ME]

Glossary of Terms & ResoQurces

- Zappos   https://infomgmt.wordpress.com/2010/02/20/the-story-zappos-com-sends-flowers-to-its-customer/
- Tools for fighting big companies https://fairshake.com/how-it-works/
- Tools for company contacts   https://www.elliott.org/company-contacts/
- Government agencies that can help- https://www.consumerfinance.gov https://www.ftc.gov

- DMV quote sourcehttps://www.yelp.com/biz/department-of-public-safety-tulsa?osq=Departments+of+Motor+Vehicles

TSA Stat - https://abcnews.go.com/US/tsa-fails-tests-latest-undercover-operation-us-airports/story?id=51022188

Nordstrom Handbook - https://www.businessinsider.com/nordstroms-employee-handbook-2014-10

Comcast story - - https://billfixers.com/blog/21-times-comcast-worst-company-america

Comcast profitable and yet bad at CX https://www.complaintsdepartment.com/comcast/

To see your flight status - https://flightaware.com/

McDonald - https://www.consumeraffairs.com/food/mcd.html?filter=none

Average American will wait for 43 https://www.marketwatch.com/story/the-average-american-will-spend-43-days-of-his-life-on-hold-2016-02-04

www.ingramcontent.com/pod-product-compliance
Lightning Source LLC
LaVergne TN
LVHW071218060725
815467LV00018B/1604